THROUGH MY EYES

UNO

SMITHA PILLAI

Made with ♥ on the Notion Press Platform
www.notionpress.com

Contents

Contents

The Why & How

The written word has always been my friend, the spoken word not that much. I prefer to stay in the shadows, in between unopened newspapers, leaves of old musty books in a library, in the silences. This is the reason why I find my peace and also my succor in this form - poetry. If you ask me what caused me to start writing, it was thoughts that I was not ready to speak about, perhaps may have been considered an outcast at school and in the larger society. But the questions I had, the observations I made, the inferences I drew, the dreams that recurred, all of these have been part of my poems. They lack the rhyme but have the reason to start a small evocative revolution in you.

1. The Soul to the Sea

Every measured step so lightly put
Every breath taken, so deep and scorching
Longing to feel something so mundane
Water flowing into my hands
Raindrops kissing my skin
Searing at the skin and tugging the heartstrings
Gravel crushed under
Breath wavers
Hands reach out to the next wave
Forcing me in, body and soul
Did I expect the sea to behave like my faucet?
Did I expect the waters to calm and soothe me?
Sing me a lilting tune
A few bars to keep me crooning
A day, a week, …Changeover to a new epiphany

Every drop stretched time
Every moist stretch of skin burned
Waiting for the next surge, the next ember to burst forth to flames
Wave upon wave,
Just water running through..So what
Crushing every inch, smothering every breath
Toes crawl in…hold on
Pushing weight back…dry land ahoy
Skin wants to melt and be one with the flow
Soul flies away drawing the horizon in
Did I sign away my control?
Did I walk away from structure?
Singing me an ode
A thousand symphonies keep me awake
An age, a lifetime…..The sea is me..soulmates don't changeover

2. Patchwork Quilt

Opening my eyes to life,
I was gifted a brand new quilt
No hand-me-downs, no refurbished ones
A new, soft, warm and fits-me-to-size quilt

I snuggled into its warm haven on cold nights
Could pull it over to hideaway
Sometimes giggles, sometimes tears, sometimes fear and sometimes wrath
Enough to cover me whole, still allowing me to flex my hands, head and legs at will

Years past, I outgrew my quilt
Parents sewed in extensions in the same fabric
Clean and neat, never feeling the joints
Still felt one, still felt whole

• 4 •

With a few more autumns, my struggles with the quilt increased
The once tight fabric loosened, gave way to breaches
I learnt to sew bright colored fabric on the outside
Yet, saw the scars on the inside every time I sought to cover my eyes

With time, the motley patches covered my quilt
Leaving little of the old fabric
The patchwork rough around the edges
Some with multiple sew-ins, heavier, uglier now

Should I give up on my quilt?
Should I get something brand new?
It's still comfy, still warm
Though it may seem all worn out and patched

But it's mine,
Every live thread sewn into place by my hands
Some amateur some pro,
Some dyed in tears, some in blood

Will I ever pass it down
Will I keep it as testament
It's my cover, my second skin
Let it burn to ashes with me

When the embers kiss the seams
You'll see the colors burst forth
You'll see the forged bonds, the rivets, the cracks
You'll yet see my life unfold

3. Same Same But Different

The forced unfeeling didn't numb me
Alert to movements sounds and smells
The low gurgle and a full throated wail
Is this your prestige or full act?

A crown of Medusa like tangles
Is all I see on the tray
Mini-me?? Staring with owl eyes
Am I still numb or is it just a trance

Not like me - her face screamed
Her light clasp on my finger
The longing eyes, the coos
Peeling me layer by layer

Days and months crawled by
Her Medusa had smoothened
Her smiles intentional
Her hands tuning familiar strings

The lines I drew around myself
Erasing them one by one she entered
Reflecting my every move, my words
She is not me - is my space violated?

Years rolled by the lines blur
She yearns to be me, but I chip away at her
Our entities are the same
Yet why do we want the same wine in a different goblet

Passions fire up- they blaze in her, mine undying embers
Emotions well up - words are hers, tears are mine
Fears creep in - my Brave front, her cowering head eggs me

The prestige is up, the act is the same
No curtains need lift
You will see me yet again
Chrysalis was me, but she is the Butterfly

4. Empty Afternoons

When the warm food descends
The afternoon sun takes a pit stop
The fans rattle in rhythm
The curtains hum along letting the warmth spread thin
When everyone just settle into their siesta
Uneasiness gets the better of me - I step out

Tip toe tip toe mental checks on the sleep meter
Slip through creaky unoiled doors
Walk up the hillock, a squirrel here, butterfly couple dancing
Touching a leaf, finding undiscovered bugs
Carefully avoiding protruding pebbles
Feeling the crunch of summer under my flip flops

Settle myself on the swing shaped branches
Pushing the earth down...just a tremor of oscillation
I smile ...not knowing why
Climb the cashew trees ..nuts n apples separate
Biting into the juicy flesh ..dripping all over
Keeping notes on clean up duties before I head back

Climbing over walls when gates are not exciting enough
Plucking gooseberries ...unclasping their arms clutching the branches
Tying up the remaining into small bundles at the hem of my frock
Scourging the ground for fallen mangoes
Saving the fruit from the red and myself from the black cousins
And time stood still for me ... Just a wish today

5. Ships in the Night

Amidst the criss cross of capillaries
I nestled my little dream
Impractical, heady childlike
Meshes as sentinels denying entry to everyone

Nurtured with desire fuzziness and warmth
Levitating unattached, yet responding to every heartstrings tug
Keep the sounds down,
The Don't s ideal face value knocks on

The crevice flattens out
The niche no more
Vaporizing tufts of cotton candy
Leave on your gooey presence..that you once were light and sweet

No dancing in gay abandon upon rooftops in the rain
No letting the hair strands free
No humming away a lost note
Clamped to the Now - No sailing on the moon

Did I unmesh my nest ?

Did I brand my quest a mirage before the sea gulls cried ?

Did I let it pass me by unglanced ?

Like ships in the night

6. A Piece of Love

Of sweaty palms
Shoes drawing patterns on the sand
Stealing glances and knotted cloth
A racing heart and silences to fill, alien territory yet tugs

A flower one day, a bouquet another
A book I cherish
A movie I longed for
Of drives and rides together, awkwardness to familiarity

Hesitant holding of hands
Of spaces disappearing
Of shared meals and fears
Pitches for post-paid bills from pre-paid, layers upon layers unfolding

Piecing together our story
Of once lost and found
The destiny - if you will - that binds us
Through nine lives and more, cyclicity and us

Each piece bottled up

Sifting through emptiness

They gleam through the glass

Pop the lid to find you again, no strings attached and still, it binds

7. A Little Less Loved

Never felt the warm caress of her hand on my head

Never felt safety in her warm embrace

Never heard praises from her

Never felt how a kiss from her would be

Never a fist bump or an encouraging nudge when I was faced with trials

Never got affirmation on a job well done

Never felt the need for all of the above either

Coz…

She sacrificed her joys for me

She spoke of me proudly far from my ear

She fought my battles and picked at thorns and shards on my path

She heard the unspoken words, feelings and people

She reprimanded in front and dried her tears behind closed doors

She steeled herself so that I could be steel

She let me be … me

What if I was loved outwardly a little less

She made me a little more

To stand out and be brave at that

To prepare me for the rough roads ahead

Never throwing me headlong..always lighting the way

The hand that held the torch unseen

A little less for the world…indebted for eternity

8. A Birthday to Remember

I was going to be 11... Or was it 12
Passing up the threshold of single digits and their close friend 10
I wanted it to be special
Or was it my mum who was more excited
She just learnt to bake
Already willing to go eggless for sophomore
I told her... I have lots of friends
She told me…invite them all

Introverted me...how do I invite them?
Should I just tell them at school?
Mum intervened... Parents; permission paramount
So hitched onto my bday twin..the extroverted one
Walked into big houses
Was made to wait for my friends to make an appearance
Ample time to shrink me down
They walked down spiral stairs
Hopped, skipped, jumped carefree into my presence
As in the movies

My extroverted twin dealt with the verbal invite
I mirrored her…mumbling address, date, time
Everyone nodded, everyone said yes…they'll come
Some feigned checking overbooked diaries
It was only walking distance
It was only early evening'
It was someone they called a friend

Mum busied herself in making space for the crowd
How could you cram them into a 2bhk
Cooked her heart out…must never run out
Learnt their names and wherefroms
Climbed ladders to put up the decor
Now, the wait…
I was dressed.. Still unsure
If I deserve this party
New clothes, clean and ironed
Now, the wait…

Only my extroverted twin arrived with her sister
It was her bday too
Hours ticked on..
Waiting for steps
Waiting for rustles
Waiting for anything
Nothing..
We cut the cake together
Partook of the feast
Tried to inject joy
Nothing..

Definitely did not deserve this
Definitely not my friends
Definitely I did something wrong
Definitely not my place to be
Definitely definitely definitely it's me
Friendships no more
Innocence no more
We no more
I dissolve away
Still traces…of pendulum swings, balloons, frosting
And a mumbling tear streaked face

9. Lost Star

A mushroom cloud beat down to obey…hair
Scrunched features, felt like a candy wrapper
Neat, prim, ironed to the seams .. uniform
Calves to die for, and gait like the boy next door

She never smiled…or rather that was not her demeanor
Always ready for a game
Loved to swing the baseball bat like nobody's business
Lovingly straightened out the feathers and then hit it out of the school
gates.. Sweet vengeance

She asked for a song
She asked me to sum up her marks
She smiled at me that day
She slumped her boy gait

She bid goodbye to the world they said
She could not survive the torture
She had no permission to be an athlete without degrees
She was the lost Star denied her outro

10. Not Good at Goodbyes

You have to go pay your respects
What if I never had any respect for the person?
Should I conjure up this feeling out of thin air?
Why should I fill myself with sadness?
Why should I scourge my memory disk for some iota of a shared memory,
That will redeem this person in my eyes?

There is a cloud cover dark n moss-grown
My eyelashes dripping black
Hair disarray. Coffee mugs stained. Chocolate foils strewn
Grown my being into a couch
It's a twister of what I remember of them... Image upon image, feeling upon feeling
I'm hanging at the precipice.. Do not want to let go

It's the norm they said

Wear black or was it white... Something washed out... Expressing starkness

Paint your face with loss, remorse, sympathy

Pin-drop silence..just be one of them... feel their pain..say a few empty words

A green tick in community contribution

I'm empty, feet leaden ...how can I act thus...I feel a little... But have nothing to offer back

An adorned obituary

The world is recounting their footsteps

Some real tears, some affected, some to serve a purpose

I knew them...is what I say..feigned acquaintance

Watch their works on loop..legacy marked for posterity

Moisten my eyes, a post, some references for everyone...for me..wallow under a shower

11. So What...

So I stood with my hands on my hips and looked daggers
Should I have stood hand at my back, you not knowing the knife I hold?
So I sat crossed leg in my full pants
Should I have sat with feet together and cross out you instead?
So I stood tall looking down on you
Should I cut off my inches from the top or bottom to get to eye levels?
So I raised my voice, questioned you
Should I have sealed out my anger, my rational self and tie it up in a noose?
So I stomped out of the so-called discussion (monologue at best)
Should I have treaded out like an angel letting my wings be clipped?
So I put myself above others
Should I erase my entity, bleed to let the vampires feast?
So I stopped the rod from landing on me
Should I have let my mortal self bear the testimony what my mind already bears?

Respect begets respect
Age, sex, relations, race are not pre-requisites
You let your full self out there, earn it
So what of expectations and norms - I write mine own!

12. My Kind

I talk to them
I walk with them
I live with them
But are they my kind?
I refuse to subject to walls
To dividers, to bells and whistles
To vermillion in my hair, my forehead
To drawing crucifix, or lifting my hands up…
To a black stone

I refuse to subject to invisible signs
To what the next person's great great grandfather's profession
To what the next person's ancestor's tyranny unleashed eons ago
To what revenge I can wreak on a history gone by

My kind is a Human Being
Differentiated from animal lives
Gifted and developed, thinking power
To do good and propagate good

My kind who still sees warmth in another of its own kind

Smiles and reflects smiles

Cries and reflects tears

Who loves existentially and not in pages of history or apprehensions of the future

13. Forgive

False smiles
Affected mannerism
Practiced concern
Yet sometimes human concern peaks
Someone who seized so much from me
Deserves zilch, pay back now.....tarry a Lil longer

I hear of illness
I hear of lost hope
Plea for pity
I'm tending to the same...did I let go
The knots are loosening..the mask chips away
I can possibly forgive...how does it matter

A bounce back
Awake from death knell
Time to turn a new leaf?
Strength gives fervor to malice
More of the same, no lessons learnt
Was I thinking of forgiveness? Right about turn

14. The Fall

The vertical world suddenly horizontal
A split second - realization
Shoulders free of weight - flung far away
Hands free of the mobile
Self awareness pulls me up
Clumsily, covering up, attempting a smile

Turning back the orientation of the world
Gathering up my baggage
Pointing to the cause - assuring no one of being whole
Hands bruised, legs stinging
Dusting away the remnants of the event
A fall from grace - attack of multiple gazes

I'm shook body and soul
Tears roll down, words garbled
Rein yourself in- pullback from the stupor
Not a kid anymore to cry over falls and bruises
Not a kid anymore to be helped up and about
Whose fall was it anyway??

15. Space - An Ever Changing Paradigm

It could just be about a little more
Or a little less
Or something just right
The right - only the owner deigns

It could be yours, mine or no one's
Private or public goes unchallenged
Try your hand at measuring it?
Arm-length, vacuum, invisible, light years, all-surpassing

Too close and it's dangerous
Too far and it's got no heart
But too close could be invading yet cute
And too far respectful but cold

Minimalism celebrates it
Materialism abhors
Art is of filling them with colors and patterns
Literature of relief and blank verse

Agro is precise to live and let live
Industrial to be crowded and overlapping
Elocution is about meaningful pauses
While music about filling white noise

Marveling at the universe
Emptiness is wonder and uncharted
Then why does science attempt at filling it up
With quarks, bosons, ETs and dark matter?

Space is so romantic yet insecure
Glum but relieving
The blip and miss or an eternity
Yet we give it a wide berth - the space bar
Are we afraid of it?
Yet envelop in its defensive layer
Yet confused if the glass is half full or half empty
Full or empty of what?
I leave it to you my friend?

16. Depression

Are you just a dent on my being?
One that can be fixed by pushing out from within
Something that will look unchanged
With a fresh coat of paint...twice over
Run your fingers and you still feel

Are you an impression of feet, weight fallen heavily?
Walking all over, pushing you deeper
Wait for time and you will he leveled
There are others like you joined hands in silence
A kind soul may yet fill you out, the edges

Are you sucked in by a force from within?
A fantasy land, with golden spires
Excesses and more, everything I dreamt of
Still in dreams, sucked into a wormhole
Kiss me out of slumber...I rise, a pintuck

Are you a deep ravine between jagged mountains?
Cutting deep, going ever deeper
Space less, breathless, falling
Trickling water, succor...moss grown, hope
Shake those mountains, drive that wedge...scars

Why are you not the dimple?
Lighting my smile
Why are you not that soft mud where flowers bloom?
Bringing in the rainbow with the rain
Wishing away, fighting away, resisting away

17. The Sacrifice

Fresh juicy pastures to have one's fill
Washed with soap and fresh water
Not a speck of dust, not hungry for a morsel
Sumptuous as sumptuous can be
No sheep dogs to bark at us
Traveling in luxury-padded wagons

Yet we squirm, huddle together
Odd bleats rent the night air
Some eyes glisten in the darkness
The breathing gets heavier, louder
Flared nostrils, hooves kicking
Coats fluff up goosebumps

At nightfall the scramble of legs
Bleats get louder, scaredy - a wailing
With passing days more empty spaces
Lessee noises, lesser bleat prayers
Who is next, why me, why they
What happens, when and how

Live another day - Die another hour
Why me to why not me
Is it joy to see not being chosen
Is it sorrow to see my friends bleed
While my co-herd stake to being steak
Am I content to watch on the sidelines

Will the juicy pastures hold sway
Will the wagon padding keep me safe
Will time fill the missing spaces
As I play the waiting game

18. Charms

Little shiny things
Jingling at your wrists
Peeking out of your skirt hems
Playing hide-n-seek from your first shirt button
Clutching at your love handles

Cutesy trinkets tied to your bags
Ribbon-like to your ride
Things you keep at your threshold
Your place of work, your place that pays
Charms all - special and lucky

First, just a fluke
Second, coincidence at best
Third, registered for trial
Fourth, could be a lucky charm?
Fifth to Seventh - I'll keep them close
Then on - All luck is because of you
As all things, time weathers
So does luck, wearing away from the charm
Everything with an expiration date
Chuck it in a corner, with other pasts
Quest on for a new one

I'll get a new one
I'll test a new one
It's a thing - how does it matter
What you do to things - you do to people?
Shiny charms - lost its shine - discarded souls

19. Transactions

Give and take
Sow and reap
Work and get paid
Exchange cash for kind and vice versa

Help and expect help back ....someday
Give time and expect it back...sometime
Lease out and expect the favor returned
Pawn out and pawn in

I look after you today. ...so you look after me tomorrow
I allow you to spend and I expect to get laid
I live life.....so You give me salvation
Expectations ...the currency we trade in

20. Tokenism

He was there by my side but did not hold out his hand when I fell
She came over to help me with my condition but refused to acknowledge the same
He watched me bleed, but refused to bandage me
She bought fruits for me but did not cut one up for me to eat while I was bandaged all over
He came with me to the park but kept talking on the phone
She took me shopping but I only shopped with her card
He made love to me but turned away when he was done
She vowed to be with me in sickness and health and left me a maid to carry on with

What of empty words
What of feigned care
What of inked relationship contracts
When you tally life's balance sheet
And all credits to you...
Encash those tokens with lonely hours

21. Leaning in

Waking slumber, shackled limbs
Rivets fused, lazy and stretched time
Eyelids drunken droop
But walk on I do - for another day

Tall sentinels lighting a pathway
Hedges below leaning in
Rubbing me, caressing me
Reaching out as if yearning for touch

Mornings do this to me
Romanticism of a faded age takes over
As the brightness clears the fog
Reality fawns - I laugh at myself

The shrubs only lean to escape
The canopy of the trees above
Selfishly sticking out their necks
For their rightful spotlight

22. Vantage

A meandering black tar road below
Vehicles, pedestrians, all miniature models
Moving about ...battery operated
The soft touch of raindrops brush against my preened feathers
They land harsh on the road below
Tip toeing...leaves, wires, concrete, asbestos , flesh, tar

A screech of vehicles, a soundless gasp
The models gather at the epicenter
Standstill ..a river of red ..a heady cocktail
Rain n blood, order n chaos, mundane n epic
More of us gather, to peer n wait
More of them gather, to click n post

Remnants of the event
Food for the day, the parliament in cacophony
Remnants of the event
Tit bits to take home n nibble on for days
We watch to survive another day
They watch to theorize on survival

23. Silence

It's quiet...it's calm
It's soundless...it's emptiness warm
I seek the silence within and without
I seek that deafening void

But I'm also aware of the guest I invite
The eerie soundlessness post a storm
When two swords clash in wordless banter
When destruction strikes without premonition

That silence I will not blow bugles to
Where death shrouds and anger smothers
Where words are wasted, no leaf shivers
Where life stills - vacuuming itself out

Just before the first cry rents the air
When eyes meet and a lot is said
Heartening surprises are hard to take in
Licking the fingertips of that silence I savor

24. Water Drop

Have you ever seen a waterdrop ..drop
Into an expense of its own
A tumbler of water
A puddle nestled in a pothole
Into the expanse of the sea
Into the palm of your hands holding some of its own
An accumulation of dewdrops tiptoeing its way to a meeting place

On impact...it creates a well
Shirking away bowl like away from the new entrant
The drop suddenly feeling like an alien .
Pops up ..spindle shaped sensing the animosity
So far it seemed to look up to whence it came
Now looking down to where it is destined
The sameness repels...but gravity forces ..into a non entity

25. Eyes Don't Lie

Does the spoken word lie?
The more we gather silvers..
The need for the spoken and written word comes to naught
Instruments of manipulation, deception
What we can say while meaning the exact opposite
How we can act out a part conceived under the fumes of absinthe

Our bodies can lie
Our frames can expand and shrink at will
Our lips can pucker at will
Legs can balance on stilts
Hair put up and let down
Each expressing a persona, a part, a mask

A language that cannot believe - the eyes
Hidden behind layers of kohl and glitter
Covered in shades of darkest hue still peeps out the truth
A smiling face, flashy clothes reeking of bills and pomposity
Sad eyes, no twinkling smiles, eyes drawing a blank
The strongest and humane language - the eyes

26. To Change or Not to

People say change is permanent
It's the most natural way
It's what defines growth
It's what defines survival

But does it mean ...I have to too
Im happy to be who I am
It's not like I'm not adaptable, malleable or flexible
But my core resists change

I like it when people say I'm the same
When people say I've not changed
It's easy to start where I left
It's when I feel I've been true to myself

The sun does not change
The moon just changes shapes but promises to return
The tides do still come and do not stop going
Ppl die and ppl are born

I'll let me be me

I'll let change wash my feet and retreat

I'll let no one rewrite me, resay me, remove me

I'll not hide, not bend, not retrace...just stay

27. What is the Glue

Two mortals ....
Wedded, bedded, childed
All green ticks
No AIs awaiting
Stick through life..they said
Why is there no 'try'
Why is it a law passed
Still we hear begging voices
Still we see rummaging to plaster rivets

The mortals do not question
It's BAU
Disagreements, violent breakouts, cold wars
It's BAU
Taking turns to take blame, no hint of smoke
It's BAU
Only children stand witnesses
But it's BAU too

Through the status quo
A stickiness starts
First it resists like the first kiss
Pull out ...but I belong with this adhesion
When they complete each other's words
When they act for the same cause
When they leave unwritten love notes around
the home
When they catch the other in an adorable moment
The glue gets thicker
Still covering up imperfections perfectly

28. Rabbit Holes

Tears, remorse, guilt, - my cup runs over
Did anyone see? Did anyone hear?
I need to keep away, unseen, unheard
Somewhere dark, somewhere deep

I paint smiles, I paint joy, I paint neutrality
Control the salt waves...let it glisten, not run over
I shroud myself in anonymity
Let the cover be transparent, thin, skin like

Pivot away...to nonsense, empty laughter
Anything to steer away my battered ship to the shore
Walk away...leave the melee..leave the scene
Bury myself deep, stay put, wait it out

Rabbit holes all
Abandoned homes of the depressed
Spiraling conch shells, deserted tunnels
Succor for the lost me

Can't I be the pupa...
Enveloped by strands of the darkness
Reinventing, rejuvenating, a retreat
The cut myself open n fly away anew

29. Walking the Dark Line

A rustle, a hoot
Crickets playing the fiddle
Toads mating calls
A flap, a crunch of dry crisps of leaves
Blindfolded careful steps
Trace a black line..to somewhere

No posts to landmark
No guardrails to stem the wandering
No limits to somewhere
The moon leads the way
Shadows play with the freaky mind
A glistening drop catches the moonbeam.. To anywhere

Stillness is calming they say
The night awakens the gray
For the always black.. What's that shade
The pull to melt away, be nothing
The longing to keep walking to eternity
Darkness swallows.. Now everywhere

30. I Met a Stranger

Some people pass by you everyday without batting an eyelid
Some people pass by you, seemingly side eyeing
Some pass by you turn a corner and look back when you are not looking
Some pass by you oblivious of anyone/anything around
Some pass a sweeping glance, not necessarily judgemental
Some pass with a nod, a smile sometimes, an easing of muscle perhaps, pace slowing
Some do the same but rush away, having ticked off the humane tracker
Some talk to you in passing
Fewer stop and talk
A handful stop, talk and walk with you

All of the above are not necessarily strangers
Some acquaintances, so called friends, some friends, some colleagues
Some blood ties near and far
Some ties thicker than blood
They all do not matter
But they all exist, share the space briefly or otherwise and move on

31. Disallowed Love

It was cliched
It was destined
It was disallowed
It was shrouded

And yet…
Longing is oft unrestrained
A glance helo longer
A graze flowing into a touch
Arhythm, a snowball fight, shared tears
Our stories retold

Under the envelope of friends
We find curtains, closed doors, shadows
We find off-camera-focii
We find songs to speak our language
We find others to relay our truth untold

As I become him
He becomes me
As we reflect off of each other
The world celebrates our saga
And yet we are disallowed

32. Heads bent down

Look around you
Every head bent down
Willingly, proudly
Not hanging in shame
Not out of respect
Not to get away with reprimand
Not inward looking
Not at a flower in the mid
Not at a child smiling on
Not at a pup passing by
Not following a tumbleweed tumble by
Not at the morsel that will keep you alive
Not at a dog eared book page
Not sifting through a newspaper
Not at a cockroach sneaking in
Not at the watch to catch the sands of time

• 53 •

Heads bent to a screen
As time and life passes you by
You capture everything
You seemingly live life
You seemingly know what it takes
You seemingly admire beauty
You allegedly express all emoti(c)ons
You allegedly serve the world
From an interface… a medium
Through a medium
For a medium…heads bent down

33. Reciprocate

What stops you from blowing that kiss back?

What makes you fold in when someone says 'I love you'?

What pulls you away when someone hugs you?

What retraces your steps when someone looks lingering on into your eyes?

What fakes a laugh when you are showered praise?

What eats your sentences when one seeks you out frequently?

What makes you recede into a rabbit hole when you get more than you desired?

Guilt

Guilt to be more

Guilt to have more

Guilt to deserve more

Guilt to expect more

Guilt of an excess … the limits to which we set too tight

Fence it up with barbed wire, broken shards and tasers

Pull down that humble stance
Pull down that fence
Imbibe, take in, savor, celebrate who you are
You don't have to shut yourself in and party
You don't have to replay the moment on loop with no audience
Reciprocate instead

34. The Blow - Up

Zero-in on 'x'
Get the means to the end 'x'
Acquired 'x'
Now get it to Capital X
Then blow it up…
Smiles seeing the sparkling shards
Tear up a little - Customary
Fix that tie, dust off the stardust
Now let's go get 'y'....

35. A Piece of Big Bang

It starts with glares...shooting spears hitting nothing

Silences, stomping feet, cutlery clanking,

Sharp quick forceful actions

Breathing breaking the silence ceiling

Nostrils flared, eyes bloodshot, gnashing teeth

Doors banged shut, faucet in full

Stereo blaring,

Contain it, release it. Plucking the petals out

One word, an act, a response to stimuli

Heaving hearts, veins throbbing, temples sweating

Closing out the distances with definitive intent

Voices slashing silence, flesh, bone and shared memories

Blames hurled, sentence syntaxes post mortem, graves dug - filled - redug

Sleeves rolled, pushed back, loose ends tied

Eventual meltdown in sight - prolong it or finish it flared

Scene heavily pregnant to explode

The first contact established - slap, slash, collars, punch
Black eye, capillaries daring to break out of knuckles
Buttons flying, ripping curtains, fabric straining
One bout done, waiting for the gong -
An advanced step, a poison dart of words
Biding times, magazines flipped, licking wounds
War cries, tears, clutching at pounding hearts
Call for Time out - sense prevails - life endures

36. Wayside Potted Plant

Lowered deftly into a well of earth
The smell of metallic paint from below engulfed
Honks, voices, whizzing motors, trailing wheels
The sun beating on me and water splashing all over
A new life, a new abode - I'm blessed

With days ambling on
No one stopped to quench my thirst
The paint was caked and crusted
People shirked me
An outcast, with no family - must grow on

With rains and occasional fizzy drinks chucked
I lived on
Longing for company I entangled hair, straps and cloth ends
To be only snapped or cut off strings at the company end
Visits gave me a facelift
Only to be abandoned as the cavalcade passed by me

My siblings separated at birth meters away
I dropped my leaves, cannibalized to survive
The green turned to black, the leathery into gaunt
Still dared to flower every month
Lest a sad soul casts a weary look on their journey on

If I could bring that eye relief
If I coils lighten that aching heart
If my ability to survive and battle on,
Instilled hope - even if a mote worth
My life is fulfilled as a wayside potted plant

37. Let there be Darkness

Shadows lengthen…
The warmth ceases
The bright orb nestles into the sea
The darkness is about to take over
Shadows grow and merge into their eternity

I squirm, peer through my leathery wings
Scratch my pointy ears, adjust positions
The branches heaving with day birds nestling back
Leaving my stronghold, I flap around the tree-
Warming up for the night ahead

Concentric circling opening to larger radii
I chart out -- Blinding lights
Struggling to adjust I retreat
Perhaps it was just cloud cover
Perhaps the night has not taken hold

Back I go questioning my understanding of time yet again
No darkness the night holds
Crackling yellow-white orbs everywhere
Lighting up the night
Just the same

I beg for my skies of the night
My portion of the darkness
To fly around in gay abandon
To merge my black with the grey environs
I was promised a time of my own - Alas

For me and the children of the night
A silent plea I table
Let night be night and day be day
The circadian rhythm will wreak havoc
Drink up the night to savor the day

38. Lights Out

Asked to form separate queues
Strangely no-one following - queue or firing line
Blinders on, walls separating
Waiting for something forward or hearing from behind
Walk-on they said

Having touch-checked around - nothing sentient
Ears do not pick any vibration except mine
Heaving breath, footsteps on marbled floors
Clothes rubbing against walls, against skin
Dared the blinders off - Light out to Lights out

Smooth silken walls pushing you ever inward
Retraced a few steps, Hollered… no one
Not one pinpoint of light
Caged all four sides, unending expanse forward and backward
Held breath to feel company - animate/inanimate, anything?

How much time elapsed?
How many more in this darkness?
How many more steps to a glimmer
Stopped, sat, wrapped in myself
Streaming tear, streaming the haloed life lead

A slow humming, a flutter of scales
Alight on my saline face
A twinkle then off - slipping between reality and illusions
A glow worm - pinching myself to realism
Push the lights out of you, let your hope orbs lead yourself on

39. Apologies

To the hugs not given
To the kisses not returned
To the open palms I did not clasp
To the smiles not acknowledged
To the moist eyes I did not wipe away
To the forward steps I took backward

The goodbyes I did not turn back to
The please I did not heed to
The sorrys I unlisted
The thank yous I felt hollow
The welcomes I swept under the doormat
The excuses i treated as that - excuses

This is the sum total of me
Would I apologize for who I am?
Or turn back time to redress
To amend the so-called wrongs
Unapologetically will continue doing just the same
I acknowledged - turn that bottle now.

40. No Crows in My City

The sleeping-in rooster crows post day break
The population of pigeons take flight
The blind bat finds succor in air conditioners
The lone bulbul hides in manicured hedges
Sparrow survivors make a comeback
The carrion eagle hovers never touching down
But crows - they made the quiet exit

Where beauty takes precedence
Where the harsh tones have no audience
Where the tilted look is ominous
Where the parliament is denied power
The dark shiny flapping wings are missed
The dissonance of caws
The rhythmic hoppers looking intently no more

Is this the crow forsaken desert
Is this the city which refuses to learn
Custodians of our ancestor lives
Has history turned back it's wing
Darkness leaves, begetting the real dark

41. Promise of Delusion

When you blow those bubbles out
Struggle to fill up balloons
Stare at diamonds on leaf tips
Pluck a dandelion in the wind
Hold a gaze in a crowd

Mayhaps you believed in the illusion
The first time - But again?
Their effervescence is the fetish
Seeking out joy in the transient
And keeping the promise of delusion alive.

42. Homestead

One day the wind will change..
What it is to my mother, the pine, if I stay still?
What it is to my sibling acorns, if I do not budge?
What it is to clover, if I do not shift my weight for her flower to bloom?
What it is to the soil below, if I stay put?

One day the wind will change,
I will be taken south,
I will linger on sunny lands,
Smell the rhododendrons, find friendly acorns
Friends who will let me be
Revel in the glory of the grey

The wind came one day
Towards the south, towards the south
Voices called out, fare thee well
Don't want to look back anymore
I'm heading south, I'm heading for my due

No sunny lands, No rhododendrons

No shriveled acorns, No tongues to reprimand

No glory, No me

But, just dreams of a colder place

Of family and bonhomie

One day the wind will change..

One day the wind will take me home

43. Let Them Flow

From the icy haunts they were born
Little rivulets
Still part snow, part fluid
Starting to course an adventure

Scraping over boulders
Tumbling over ledges
They are allowed to sprinkle, to veer, to rush, to smear
In abandone lessons still come abegging

As the greys give way to greens
The stones they no longer bruise, they only silhouette
The flow loses speed to inquisitiveness
To meander into unknown lands, t linger even

The trees, they stop them moving inland
The undergrowth warns them to stay the course
Sentinels, guardrails to contain
To keep them to the beaten path

The rivulets are mighty rivers now
Fluid memories adding to their body
Finding ways to spread their might
Damming themselves they break into rivulets again

Adventurous journeys no more
Some quench the parched earth and lose their entity
Some wind into still lakes
Some allow themselves to be muddied and cloggy

Still some break the shackles
Hastened by water memories and dreams
To still bring them to fruition
To be one with the sea

44. The Mortal Seraphim

With snowflakes drifted a cherub
Asleep.. unaware...blissful
Softly descending..the wings shriveled
The purplish aura fading, the face shown ablaze
With fervent rubbing when he opened his droopy eyes
A la earth, a mortal abode

Nurtured and nourished by earthly beings
Wonderstruck eyes...wide smiles in his wake
Touching every leaf, flower, life and rock
Embossing the purplish hue
Playing the lute and singing lilting tunes
Still incomplete..the cherub longed for the song

Treading on fallen leaves
Chanced upon an old forgotten tune
The notes, the words, the bars in disarray
Need to set it right...Can I do it alone?
With hesitant eyes and cherubic smiles
Came forth 6 more of his kind

The spell broken
The feathers unfurl
The halos return
The notes re-arrange
The song is complete
And so is the rainbow

Acknowledgements

While the Thank you list is endless, I would like to still pen it down for my own RIP.

To start with, my parents, who had seeded the book bug in me, taught me the written and the spoken word. My language teachers in school who have forever encouraged me to write reams and reams despite the marks they carry. My friends at every turn who have written with me, shared, criticized and dreamt up a world where we all could be lauded writers. My kids who have allowed me my voice in their scholastic writings. Always complaining that it's difficult to pass this off as their writing but never crumpling them up for the dust bin. To the extended family who have encouraged me and believed in me.

Thank you to my corporate writing club for rekindling the joy of writing as life, kids and profession took center stage. Cannot leave out BTS for getting me to believe that self care was not self-ish.

Thank you Notion for providing such an easy to use platform to get my aspirations in print.

Last but not the least, I would like to thank my husband for being such a torchbearer and support to me.not letting me lose my entity in the humdrum of responsibilities and everyday life.

Appendix

While poetry is open to interpretation by the reader, would also love to provide the PoV of the author here on each of the pieces. This is an attempt to bring the original thought when the piece was created. But this should not stop the reader from filling in their own color, reminiscing their own experiences and shining a new light on these writings -

- **The Soul to the Sea:** The difference in response to a crush Vs a soulmate
- **Patchwork Quilt:** A nutshell of my life so far and despite what transpired would I have it any other way
- **Same Same But Different:** This was written for my daughter when she turned 5
- **Empty Afternoons:** My summer vacations as a child in Kerala
- **Ships in the Night:** Of Undone Dreams
- **A Piece of Love:** The journey I share with my equal half
- **A little less loved:** Mother's love
- **A Birthday to Remember:** Self-explanatory, but something which makes me detached in friendships
- **Lost Star:** An ode to a school friend who is no more
- **Not good at good byes:** My struggle with bereavement calls
- **So what...:** Pure anger
- **My Kind:** My answer to political views
- **Forgive:** Forgiveness does not come easy
- **The Fall:** An account of a physical fall on a busy road
- **Space - an ever changing paradigm:** Self explanatory
- **Depression:** Being literal
- **The Sacrifice:** The insider's view of corporate lay-offs

- **Charms:** Of changing affections
- **Transactions:** The trade of life
- **Tokenism:** Self explanatory
- **Leaning in:** Of false best friends
- **Vantage:** A crow's PoV on a road accident
- **Silence:** What I like/dislike about silence
- **Waterdrop:** The struggle to be different Vs follow the world
- **Eyes Don't Lie:** The language of eyes
- **To Change or Not To:** Struggle with change
- **What is the glue:** My take on what keeps a marriage
- **Rabbit Holes:** Self explanatory
- **Walking the dark line:** My love for literal darkness
- **I met a stranger:** When relationships change starkly
- **Disallowed Love:** An Ode to the love story I swear by
- **Heads bent down:** To the scrolling age
- **Reciprocate:** A call to my introverted self
- **The Blow up:** Today's goals
- **A piece of Big bang:** How we carry the violence of what created us
- **Wayside Potted Plant:** Just plants that I see on the pavements and my take on what their animated being would feel
- **Let there be darkness:** The struggle of nocturnal animals in a city of lights
- **Lights out:** The cycle of birth and death
- **Apologies:** Regrets but not ready to change yet
- **No crows in my city:** Self explanatory
- **Promise of Delusion:** The delulu is my solulu age
- **Homestead:** A letter to a stubborn friend
- **Let Them Flow:** Animated water bodies
- **The Mortal Seraphim:** Fangirling